Brooklyn Cats

Joan Cofrancesco

authorHOUSE®

AuthorHouse™
1663 Liberty Drive
Bloomington, IN 47403
www.authorhouse.com
Phone: 1 (800) 839-8640

Published by AuthorHouse 08/28/2017

ISBN: 978-1-5462-0654-5 (sc)
ISBN: 978-1-5462-0666-8 (e)

Print information available on the last page.

"There is no true beauty without a little strangeness in the proportions."

--francis bacon

brooklyn cats

bottle of brooklyn lager
joint and
concerto for two violins
memories of bach
in the air

"to get
to brooklyn
from manhattan
we have to go under
the east
river" she said
"do you mind"

riding the d
to the
brooklyn museum
to see
basquait
who used to
graffiti
these trains

used bookstore in brooklyn
a black cat
dreaming
beside a first edition
of
apollinaire

black tie shirt
silver chain
tight jeans
& brooklyn swagger

smell
leather
feel your sweat
believe me
i have no regrets
about our fucking
subway ride

there is nothing better
than walking into
a used bookstore
in brooklyn
on a rainy afternoon

drinking
mimosas
in the morning
in brooklyn
what a great way
to start

we tap the dragons
on the sides of our purple goblets
together
in an unmade bed
fog will be here
by morning
he waits tables
at a café
in soho
crosses the hudson
every evening
climbs to his small
room in brooklyn
and writes poems
into the midnight

brooklyn
hooded sweatshirts
pass out pot
turbaned cab drivers
drive past

wake up
hear *let it be*
read li po
and see basquait

he calls me SAMO

i am basquiat's
cat my black
fur matted
like dreadlocks
i am basquiat's
cat
sitting on andy warhol's
lap
getting painted
blue
pawing at his brush
as he scribbles
words
across
the canvas
jiving
to hiphop
pissing
on silkscreens
licking empty
campbell's soup
cans

sake
haiku
haiku
haiku
sleep

middle of upstate ny summer
i buy wool socks and sake

other than lovers
life is one gargoyle
after another

for a poet
loneliness can be one hell
of a companion

whose smile is wider
wcw or the plum?

rodin's thinker's butt
moons me

light snow falling
on the birches
i'll be leafless soon

japanese poetry
alone in my room
long cold upstate winter
flies by

paris
19th century poets
who knew how to write about life

my rice paper journal
daily enlightenment

hot night
ruby tuesday
playing
stars fireflies
a woman singing
above a garage

li po says it all
in 2 lines

death walked in
my one bedroom apartment
sat next to me on the bed
"illusions" i said
and watched the sunset

weed
beer
bukowski
bathtub bubbles

basho & li po
frog & toad

i call
my yellow and blue paintings
vancassos

bukowski makes me
want to smoke drink
fuck and write a poem
all at the same time

in my true religion jeans
smoking a joint
at 3 in the morning
learning how it's done
from a meditating daddy longlegs

hunters?
venison, yup;
verlaine, huh?
rifles, uh-huh!
rimbaud, what?
walmart, beer,
nothing else matters

peace
driving my open mg
afternoon sun
down rt. 20 in ny
new shades
& vivaldi on

bukowski
whiskey
whores or muses
cats horse track
haunted

meditation
a cushion
for a sore mind

the karma of past lives
without the memories

in college
i learned to eat
bologna sandwiches
and drink genesee beer

incense
cat on cushion
nothing to do

love is
hard to wash off
even with turpentine

lost and stuck
in the strange city
of my birth

she likes turkey beer
and expensive perfume
loves foreign films
and art galleries
but hates museums
she says they make her fart

in my pocket
poems of reverdy
becoming paintings
of picasso

paris afternoon
if i didn't have a leica
would i remember?

naked beach bodies
all as horny as molly bloom

so hot
i'm panting
like a st. bernard
saving skiers

at the laundromat
pubic hairs in the washer

rimbaud & morrison
say get deranged
i prefer butter
in the butter compartment
ironed shirts & timely appointments

reading rimbaud
deranging my senses
studying colors
of vowels
drinking absinthe
listening to jim
trying to break
on through to the
other side

he had
just 2 books
a bed
a poster of farah fawcett
and was happy

arab poets
write about war
chinese poets
write about love
african poets
write about freedom
lesbian poets
stroke their cats

rainy afternoon
café in paris
contented and alone

you lather me
in the tub
we drink wine
smoke pot
and listen to marvin gaye
old school
what a gas!

warhol in provincetown
i buy green sunglasses
and coke at the general store

today i feel as surreal
as the rising remains
of salvador dali
mustache intact

the subway screeches—
i'm alive
and back in nyc

sipping apricot brandy
it's snowing
fat white cats outside

reading
my black cat "guinness"
purring beside me

a bottle of merlot
in the park
let's have a renoir picnic
with umbrellas and clouds

i'm in someone's dream
annointed with oil
talking to cavafy
in a café in alexandria
he goes to sleep
and i wake up

i scribble
draw then dab
with india ink
one black dot
in the middle of the page
period

in high tech sneakers
and drake t-shirt
cutting a small steak
by candlelight

top 5

eiffel tower at sunset
minke whales breeching
beatles performing
santorini sunset
you naked on my brass bed

winter night
my cat warming himself
against the bulb
in my plastic buddha

ground zero
a burnt photo in the rubble

i'm as calm as
a bodhisattva
my huge black and white cats
curl together
like yin and yang

cat prowling under a full moon
my shadow
makes me want to live

i pack bly
bukowski brautigan
and a banana
and head out

i have a cat
i feel rich

in my dream
bosch creatures chase me
then thankfully
i wake up in my
modern hell

janis
in her photo at monterey
incense

i met monk merton
he said meditate more
and be careful of the wiring

after brownies & green tea
i drive my yellow vw
through the stars

30 hail marys
and 20 our fathers
worth of a fucking good time

a big orange cat
in a gondola in venice

like dylan thomas
i won't kiss death's ass

impressions of sunlight
monet goes blind

art scene
installations
traffic lights
taxidermied animal heads
shovels
lava lamps
doesn't anybody paint anymore

she smokes salem
reads tarot cards
and loves to visit
the tower where marie antoinette
was beheaded

15
st. christopher medals
in my air travel bag

62
and loving the rapper
drake
i continue
to surprise myself

mykonos
greek queens
keep cool
their feet in the water

my time
when urinals
and soup cans
finally make it
into the museum
to hang with
the renoirs

reverdy
brautigan
talking to each other
in my backpack
on a train
to brooklyn

i think andy was lonely
with his factory
full of people

she said
how can you write a book
about brooklyn
without mentioning
the bridge

in a dingy
used bookstore
in brooklyn
i see a black cat
who leads me to
a first editon of brautigan's
please plant this book
black cats
good luck

subway
behind a bag lady
and a young man
with a cello
i get off

Printed in the United States
By Bookmasters